Street Skateb

Flip Tricks

Street Skateboarding:
Flip Tricks

Evan Goodfellow
with Doug Werner

Photography by
Tadashi Yamaoda

Tricks performed by Evan Goodfellow
and friends

Tracks Publishing
San Diego, California

TRACKS
PUBLISHING

Street Skateboarding:
Flip Tricks

Evan Goodfellow with Doug Werner

Tracks Publishing
140 Brightwood Avenue
Chula Vista, CA 91910
619-476-7125
tracks@cox.net
www.startupsports.com

Copyright © 2005 by Doug Werner
10 9 8 7 6 5 4 3 2

Publisher's Cataloging-in-Publication

Goodfellow, Evan.
    Street skateboarding : flip tricks / Evan Goodfellow
with Doug Werner ; photography by Tadashi Yamaoda ;
tricks performed by Evan Goodfellow and friends.
    p. cm.
    Includes index.
    LCCN 2005905034
    ISBN 1-884654-24-X

    1. Skateboarding.   I. Werner, Doug, 1950-
II. Title.

GV859.8.G662 2005   796.22
                           QBI05-600130

I dedicate this book
to my family,
friends
and the NSH.

Acknowledgements

Thanks to

Tadashi Yamaoda for performing tricks and taking the photos.

Cody Brannin,
Daryl Peirce,
Mike Remando
Steven Shippler
Tyler Surrie
and **Marius Syvanen** for performing tricks.

Jimmy Cao for performing our cover trick.

Jim Montalbano for graphic production.

Phyllis Carter for editing.

Preface

This is my second skate book, and it covers flip tricks. My first, *Street Skateboarding: Endless Grinds and Slides*, was about curb tricks. The goal of each skateboarding guide is to provide readers with the tools they need to expand their bag of tricks. Although each book deals with a separate aspect of skateboarding, it's natural to combine the two in real-world skating.

At the onset let me tell you that it is difficult to convey in words how to do tricks. I've included lots of photos to help. The captions give more information. Some tricks are easier than others. With each trick, you need to understand where your feet belong, and your muscles need to learn how to perform and follow through.

Skateboarding requires hours and hours of practice. That's the beauty of it, really — spending your time traveling to different skate spots, skating with friends and trying new tricks. I hope this book helps you learn, and that you gain an even greater appreciation for the sport.

Sincerely,

Evan Goodfellow

Warning label

Skateboarding can be dangerous. Riders should know and follow safe skateboarding procedures and wear appropriate safety gear at all times. Although the skateboarders in this book do not wear safety gear, this book, in no way, endorses riding without it.

Contents

> *Most individuals skate out of curiosity; NOT because mom or dad skate or even because mom and dad approve.*

Introduction

How do you make the board stick to your feet?

How do you make the board flip like that?

If you have asked those questions, you are in the right place. This book is intended to help skaters advance in skill level and progress in style. It should also be of interest to those simply curious about the sport of skateboarding. We wish to impart an appreciation for skateboarding as well as explain how you can make a skateboard do all those things.

Survival of the fittest

Boundaries need to be pushed and technology needs to advance in order for a sport to last and remain enjoyable for participants. The late '70s and early '80s was a period of great innovation and excitement in skateboarding. One skateboarder stood out during this era, and his influence continues to this day. Rodney Mullen created many of the tricks that comprise the foundation of performance skateboarding.

Rodney Mullen

Most individuals skate out of curiosity; NOT because mom or dad skate or even because mom and dad approve. Rodney Mullen can attest to this truth. He began skateboarding in 1977, much to the distress of his wealthy father who practiced medicine. It was several years before Rodney was able to get his first board. His dad finally consented only when Rodney promised that after his first injury, he would give it up. Well, he did not get hurt. He got good.

Rodney quickly succeeded in the world of skateboarding. He picked up a shop sponsorship within nine months after he began riding. He then entered and won contests in his home state of Florida and later in California.

> **Math and science are lame subjects for many. However, the average skateboarder does not realize that he or she is utilizing principles of math and physics with every trick.**

In 1978 Rodney Mullen managed to get serious recognition when he placed fourth against top pros at the Kona Contest in California. The following year, he won first place at the Oceanside Contest, which also gained him his first skateboard sponsor — Walker. In 1980 Rodney competed against one of the top freestyle champs, Steve Rocco, and won a close contest. This win sparked the relationship with Stacey Peralta, and soon after, Rodney Mullen began riding for Powell Peralta.

Rodney Mullen contributed to the resurgence of skateboarding in the '80s by performing in videos produced by Vision and Powell, representing the cutting edge of skateboarding. He knew all the moves and created a ton of his own. Tricks that he invented include:

Godzilla rail flip
540 shuvit
50-50 saran wrap
Helipop
Gazelle
Heelflip
Double heelflip
Impossible
Ollie impossible

Rodney Mullen contributed to the resurgence of skateboarding in the '80s by performing in videos produced by Vision and Powell, representing the cutting edge of skateboarding.

Sidewinder
360 flip
360 pressure flip
Casper 360 flip
50-50 sidewinder one-footed ollie
Backside 180 flip
Ollie nosebone
Ollie fingerflip
Airwalk
Frontside heelflip shuvit switch stance 360 flip
Helipop heelflip
Kickflip underflip
Casper slide
No handed 50-50 kickflip
Half flip darkslide
540 double kickflip
Caballerial impossible
Half cab kickflip underflip
Handstand flip
Rusty slide

> *The point is to know that there are principles behind tricks that a skateboarder can learn in order to progress.*

Rodney Mullen continues to skate, innovate and hold pro status. Intricately connected to Rodney Mullen's skateboarding is his fascination with mathematics and science. Math and science are lame subjects for many. However, the average skateboarder does not realize that he or she is utilizing principles of math and physics with every trick. Knowing these principles is essential to learning how to move and control a skateboard — like how to flick your front or back foot to make the board leave the ground; how to make the board flip or how to keep your board from sliding once it's on the curb.

It's all Greek to me

I'm not saying that a skateboarder has to be a math and science whiz. The point is to know that there are principles behind tricks that a skateboarder can learn in order to progress. Understanding the mechanics involved in flips, slides and grinds has led to many new tricks and variations of old tricks.

Science also has led to advancements in equipment. One example is the invention and introduction of urethane wheels in 1973. Skaters used to ride clay wheels that caused a clunky, slippery ride. Urethane wheels provided traction and higher speeds, which led to much greater performance. Scientific principles also have created thinner boards that allow better movement and easier flips.

Origins of flip tricks

Several years ago, I visited a very old skate park called China Creek in Vancouver B.C., Canada. This park had two really crazy bowls, and over in a corner was a circular cement pad with a curb around it. I was not impressed with the park and wondered what this little round cement pad was for. It seemed a waste of space. A fellow skater told me that freestylers congregated around the cement pad and experimented with different moves. Little did they know that their gyrations were the genesis of street skating.

Freestyle skateboarding gave birth to flip tricks. Back in the day, guys and girls wore short shorts and headbands and worked their 180s and 360s on freestyle boards. Freestyle boards were shorter and narrower, thus easier to maneuver than ramp boards. Freestylists even had areas marked off in skate parks especially for them to do their thing.

Science also has led to advancements in equipment. One example is the invention and introduction of urethane wheels in 1973.

Skateboarding is no pogo stick

The pogo stick was a common Christmas wish-list item several years ago. A pogo stick is a pole with handles and places for your feet on each side. At the end of the pole is a spring that allows the pole and rider to bounce up and down. Some people can't remember this toy because it isn't around anymore. That's because the pogo stick allowed no room for progression. On the other hand, skateboarding is moving closer to becoming an established sport because there is always room for advancement and expression.

> *Skateboarding is moving closer to becoming an established sport because there is always room for advancement and expression.*

Skateboarding is all about change and progress, and that includes its products. Skateboards keep getting lighter, stronger and faster. Manufacturers experiment with various metals and designs to create lightweight yet super strong trucks. Board makers know that skateboarders want to ride down huge sets of stairs, rails and ramps without equipment failure.

Skateboarding styles dictate equipment changes. In the early to mid '90s, skateboarders moved away from ramps and focused on curb and flip tricks. Most tricks were done on relatively low curbs and small sets of

In the early '90s there were certain skateboard videos that changed the way we skated. These videos introduced technical skateboarding — specifically flip tricks. stairs. But by the end of the decade, bigger was better. It's now common for individuals to jump down ten stairs and do a rail of equal or greater height. This change in ridable terrain influenced how companies manufactured boards.

Tricks got bigger and boards broke more often. Riders needed new boards due to a worn out tail or nose or because they didn't land properly and shattered gear. As a result, companies produced bigger and stronger boards that could sustain the stress.

> *Plan B's second video,* Virtual Reality, *demonstrated that technical flip tricks didn't have to stay on the flats but could be done on ledges, stairs, even handrails.*

Video history

In the early '90s there were certain skateboard videos that changed the way we skated. These videos introduced technical skateboarding — specifically flip tricks. They included *Blind Video Days, Plan B Questionable,* and *Plan B Virtual Reality.*

Blind Video Days

Blind Video Days started a revolution. The film was released in 1991 and showcased innovative street skateboarding. The video featured four key skateboarders — Guy Mariano, Mark Gonzales, Rudy Johnson and Jason Lee — who continued to challenge and push the envelop for years.

Guy Mariano performed lots of half cabs, manuels and nose manuels, frontside big spins and backside big spins. Tricks involving flips included kickflips, manuel kickflip out, as well as a few 360 kickflips.

Mark Gonzales performed old-school tricks like the no comply. He also included new-school tricks like shuvits and flip tricks. Mark introduced various grinds and slides as well as some rather advanced flip tricks that weren't common in videos until years later. His advanced flip tricks included a kickflip frontside

boardslide and a double kickflip. The most amazing part of the video is when Mark boardslides a double kinked handrail.

Rudy Johnson wowed many of the viewers with his ability to do 360 flips. At the end of the video during the credits, you see him perform a 360 flip melon grab off a bump. Another awesome trick was his manuel 360 flip out. At the time manuels and nose manuels were fairly common but had not been shown with a 360 flip out.

With his long sideburns and messy hair, Jason Lee showed us that just when we thought skateboarding had progressed to the limit, there was more. His section featured innovative manuel tricks including a fakie manuel and a kickflip manuel kickflip out. Jason Lee's flip trick combos included backside kickflips, a kickflip 50-50, a kickflip 5-0 tailslide and 360 flips. Most impressive was his kickflip backside tailslide.

Genius of Plan B

Another highly innovative video that changed skateboarding was the first Plan B called *Questionable*. The video featured top-name pros like Danny Way, Collin McKay, Pat Duffy, Ryan Fabry, Sal Barbier, Rodney Mullen, Mike Carroll and Rick Howard. This video included technical flip tricks like kickflip late shuvits, nollie 360 flips, nollie front flips, double heelflips, pressure flips and even advanced grinds and slides on handrails.

Pat Duffy's part in *Questionable* is one of the best video roles ever. Although he was the only amateur on

Stylish and challenging tricks live on. The harder the trick, the greater its esteem.

the filming team, he performed bigger handrails and more advanced tricks than the pro riders. Duffy's section features him doing backside smith grinds and 50-50s down massive rails including a double kink rail with no runway. The craziest is his backside lipslide down a ten-stair rail in the rain. It took most pros 10 years to catch up and match a part like this. It was no surprise that after such a performance, he turned pro.

The Plan B company was cutting edge and attracted some of the best skateboarders in the world. Like in any sport, company or art, when the best minds in the field collaborate, the results can be awesome. Plan B's second video, *Virtual Reality*, demonstrated that technical flip tricks didn't have to stay on the flats but could be done on ledges, stairs, even handrails.

Skateboarders featured in *Virtual Reality* included Colin McKay, Tony Fergusson, Sean Sheffey, Mike Carroll, Rick Howard, Pat Duffy and Danny Way. The most impressive part of the video are the many switch stance tricks that seem to be regular stance tricks. Switch stance tricks are done riding in the opposite position you normally would. It is comparable to a right-handed hockey player playing left-handed simply for the challenge.

Highlights from Colin McKay include inward varial heelflips, a switch noseslide kickflip out, a switch backside kickflip down six stairs and kickflip noseslides. The other part of Colin's performance is a revolutionary vert sequence where he applied new street tricks to vert ramp riding.

Mike Carroll does amazing tricks in this video — 360 flip to noseslide, frontside kickflip, switch kickflips, switch kickflip to manuel, nollie 180 kickflip to tailslide, and an amazing nollie flip down a big set of stairs at the EMB skate spot in San Francisco. Mike Carroll's signature trick is the frontside kickflip. He does it down stairs, over gaps and with noseslides. Rick Howard also does a great frontside kickflip to a 180 nosegrind.

Pat Duffy applies more technical aspects in *Virtual Reality* than he did in *Questionable*. He performs a 360 flip noseslide, 360 flip tailslide, 360 flip to lipslide down a six-stair rail, a nollie heelflip and a switch kickflip both down six stairs, and most impressive of all, a 360 flip noseblunt slide on a curb. In the slam section, you see Pat almost land a 360 flip noseblunt slide

on a ledge going down ten stairs.

The last section of *Virtual Reality* features Danny Way in a stunning performance. He performs nollie frontside heelflips, a switch kickflip tailslide, a switch kickflip 5-0, a switch nose manuel fakie flip out, and large 360 flips. The two best tricks are his switch noseslide down a ten-stair handrail and a nollie kickflip down a grass gap at Carlsbad High School. Danny Way's section is amazing because he does technical tricks on curbs and attempts them down handrails and stairs.

Over the years, kickflips, heelflips and 360 flips have remained key. Other tricks like the ollie impossible and the pressure flip have faded with little hope of being revived. Stylish and challenging tricks live on. The harder the trick, the greater its esteem.

Flip tricks

1 Kickflip

1. Snap the tail against the ground like you would for an ollie.

2. Your front foot should be turned at a slight angle and in the middle of the board.

3.As you snap the tail, jump up with the board and flick your front foot to the side.

4.As the board spins, keep both feet above the board while it completes the flip.

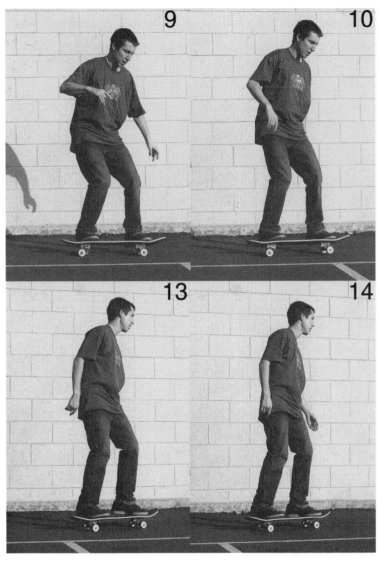

5. Once the board has completed the flip, land on the board bending your legs as you hit the ground to absorb the impact.

The secrets to kickflips are to flick the board during the ascent and to keep your feet above the board at all times.

2 Switch kickflip

1. Snap the tail against the ground like you would for an ollie.

2. Your front foot, turned at a slight angle, should be in the middle of the board.

3. As you snap the tail, jump up with the board and flick your front foot to the side.

4. As the board spins, keep both feet above the board while it completes the flip.

5. Once the board has completed the flip, land on the

board bending your legs as you hit the ground to absorb the impact.

The secrets to switch kickflips are to flick the board on the ascent and to keep your feet above the board at all times.

3 Heelflip

1. Snap the tail against the ground like you would for an ollie.

2. Your front foot should be placed in the middle of the board with your toes slightly over the edge.

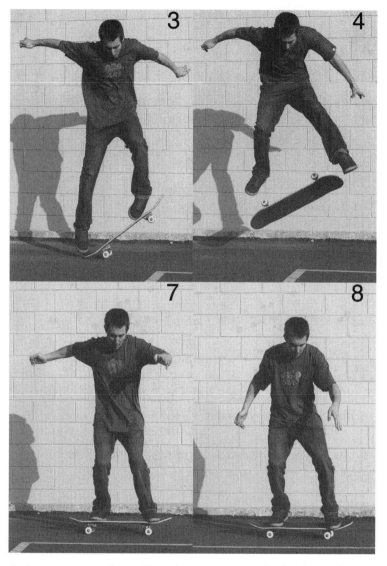

3. As you snap the tail and jump up with the board, kick your front foot straight across the board to make it spin.

4. The spin happens when the ball of your foot hits the edge of the board.

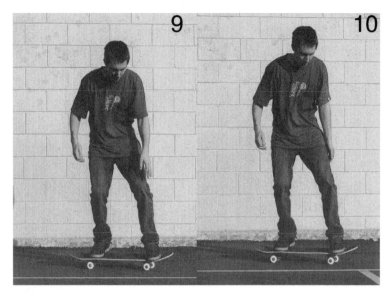

5. When your front foot extends, bring it back up over the board so that both feet are above the board as it flips.

6. As the board completes its flip, you should be descending.

7. Place your feet back on the board as it falls to the ground and bend your knees to absorb the impact.

The secret to heelflips is to remember that the ball of your foot makes the board spin, not your heel.

4 Switch heelflip

1. For switch tricks, you stand in the opposite position than normal. That is, if you are regular-footed, stand goofy on the board. If you are goofy-footed, stand regular.

2. Place your back foot (normally your front foot) in the middle of the tail. Your front foot should be in the middle of the board with your toes a bit over the edge.
3. Snap the tail and kick your front foot straight out so that the board begins to flip. It may be easier to angle

your front foot and shoulders slightly inward.

4. When the board flips, make sure to keep your feet above the board and to land on top of it as it descends.

5. Bend your knees to absorb the shock of landing.

The secret to this trick is to make sure your front foot kicks so that the ball of your foot causes the board to flip.

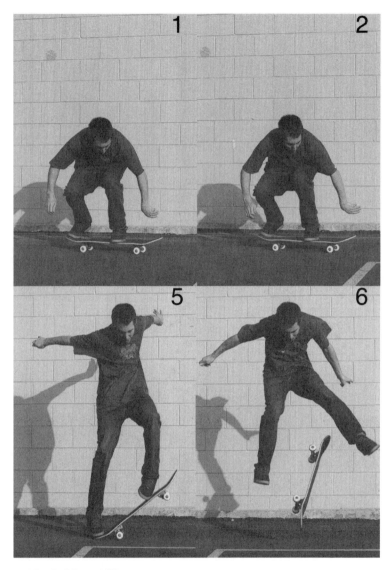

5 Varial heelflip

1. Place your back foot on the edge of the tail. If you
are riding regular, it is the left side of the tail. For goofy-
footed, it will be the right side.

2. Your front foot should be placed with your toes

slightly hanging over the edge like a heelflip.

3. As you snap the tail against the ground, you want to scoop it out in front of you so that the board does a varial (a 180 of the board, not your body).

4. As the board begins to turn, kick your front foot

straight out as if you were doing a heelflip. The heelflip helps the board turn the remainder of the 180.

5. As the board spins and flips, keep your body straight so you can land with both feet on the board.

6. Land with both feet on the board with knees bent for absorption.

The secret for varial heelflips is to time the varial with the heelflip. Begin the heelflip a split second after you snap and scoop the tail.

6 Switch varial heelflip

1. Place your back foot on the edge of the tail. If you skate regular, it will be the left side. For goofy foots, it will be the right side.

2. Your front foot should be placed with your toes

hanging slightly over the edge — like a heelflip.

3. When you snap the tail against the ground, scoop it out in front of you so the board does a varial (a 180 of the board — not body).

4. As the board begins to turn, kick your front foot

straight out as if you were doing a heelflip. The heelflip helps the board turn the remainder of the 180.
5. While the board spins and flips, keep your body straight so that you land with both feet on the board.
6. Descend with both feet on the board and bend your knees for absorption.

The secret for switch varial heelflips is to time the varial with the heelflip. Start the heelflip a split second after you snap and scoop the tail.

7 360 flip

1. Place your back foot on the edge of the tail just where it begins to turn up. For the regular-footed, it will be the right edge of the tail; and for goofy, it will be the left edge.

2. Place your front foot in the kickflip position.

3. As you snap the tail, scoop your back foot behind you as hard as you can. This scooping will produce the 360 spin.

4. As your board begins to spin, flick your front foot to

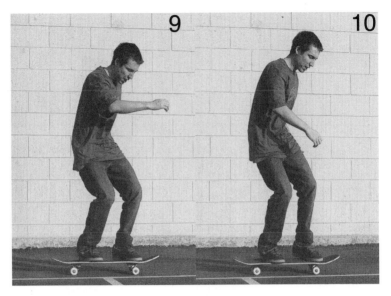

the side of the board to help the flip.

5. As the board spins and flips, your feet should be above the board.

6. Descend and land with both feet on the board with your knees bent to absorb the shock.

The secrets to 360 flips are to scoop your back foot and to flick your front foot slightly.

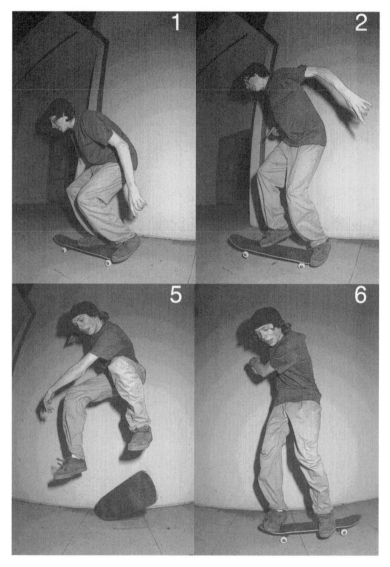

8 Fakie 360 flip

1. Begin by riding backward.

2. Place your back foot on the edge of the tail right where the tail begins to turn up. For regular-footed skaters, it will be the right edge of the tail; and for

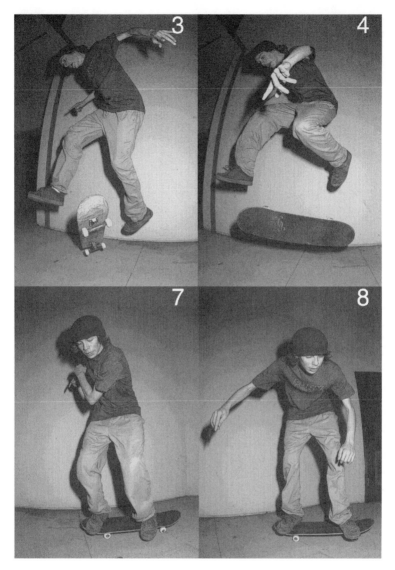

goofy, it will be the left edge.

3. Place your front foot in the kickflip position.

4. When you snap the tail, scoop your back foot behind you as hard as possible. This scooping will produce the 360 spin.

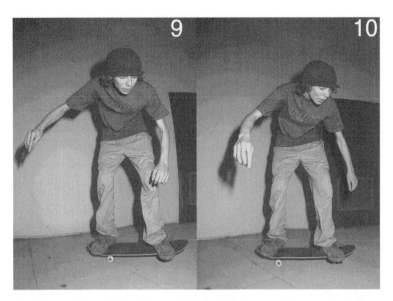

5. As your board begins to spin, flick your front foot to the side of the board to cause the flip.
6. Keep your feet above the board.
7. Land with knees bent.

The secrets to fakie 360 flips are the scooping of your back foot and the slight flick of your front foot.

9 Backside half cab kickflip

1. Place your back foot in the middle of the tail. Your front foot should be in the kickflip position.
2. Snap the tail and as the board ascends, turn your shoulders and feet so that your body and board

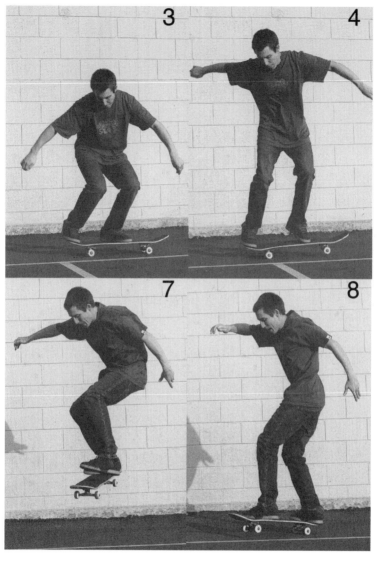

begin a 180.

3. Flick your front foot so that your board does a kick-flip.

4. The 180 degree starts it and the kickflip should be done by the time the board has turned 180.

5. As the board flips, keep your feet above it.
6. Land with knees bent.

The secret to this trick is in the half cab. Learn the half cab ollie and kickflip first.

10 Frontside half cab kickflip

1. Place your foot near the edge of the tail. For the regular-footed, place it on the left side. For the goofy-footed, place it on the right side.

2. Your front foot should be in middle of the board at

about a 45-degree angle.

3. Begin riding backward and place your feet in the above mentioned position.

4. Snap the tail against the ground. You must lean over the board so it doesn't shoot out in front of you.

5. As you snap the tail, turn your shoulders and flick your foot across the board while bringing your foot around to the front. The ollie, the turn of your shoulders and the flick of the board, should cause the board to turn 180 and flip.
6. When you turn, be sure to pull your legs up so the board can flip underneath you.
7. Descend and place your feet back on the board with knees bent.

The secrets to this trick are the shoulders and the flick of the kickflip. As you snap the tail, you should be turning your shoulders. The kickflip should begin as soon as your body begins turning.

11 Backside half cab heelflip
1. Place your front foot on the left side of the tail for regular and the right side for goofy.
2. Your back foot should be at a 90-degree angle with your toes hanging slightly over the edge.

3. Ride forward, snap the nose and in one fluid motion turn your shoulders and kick your front foot out and around to the front of the board.

4. The kick of the board will be like a heelflip, except instead of kicking straight out, kick your foot out and

around to make 180 degrees.

5. Turn with the board during the 180.

6. Remember to land with your knees slightly bent for absorption.

The secret to half cab heelflips is to kick your back foot out and around so that the board does a 180.

12 Frontside half cab heelflip

1. Riding fakie, place your back foot on the tail with your toes near the front edge of the tail.

2. Your front foot should be in the middle of the board with your toes hanging slightly off the edge.

3. Snap a fakie ollie and bring your front foot around with the board.

4. As you snap the board, begin turning your shoulders.

5. When your board and body begin turning, kick your front foot out across the board so that the ball of your

foot makes the board flip.

6. While the board spins and flips, bring your feet up so that you do not interfere with its rotation.

7. Land with both feet on the board and knees bent.

The secret to this trick is popping a good fakie 180 so that board is in the air long enough to turn and flip.

13 Nollie kickflip

1. Place your front foot in the middle of the nose of the board.

2. Your back foot is halfway between the middle of the board and the back bolts. Your back foot should

be at a 90-degree angle.

3. Snap the nose on the ground like a nollie and bring your front foot and board forward.

4. As the board ascends forward, take your back foot and flick it to the side and backward in order to flip

the board.

5. The board should be spinning underneath you. Make sure to keep your feet above the board.

6. Descend and land on the board. Bend your knees and prepare for impact.

The secrets to this trick are to bring the board forward during the nollie and to kick your foot to the side and back. This provides the proper amount of tension between forward and backward so that the board is able to flip under you.

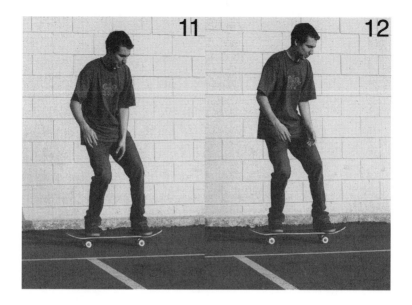

14 Fakie kickflip

1. Place your back foot in the middle of the tail and your front foot at a slight angle in the middle of the board.

2. Ride backward in this position.

3. Snap the tail and as your board is coming up, flick your front foot forward and to the side. This will cause the board to flip.

4. It's easier to look backward when riding backward.

5. As the board flips, keep your feet above the board.

6. Land with both feet on the board with your knees slightly bent.

The secret to fakie kickflips is to ride looking backward. Some skaters find this trick easier to learn than kickflips where you ride forward.

15 Frontside pop shuvit (varial)

1. Place your back foot in the middle of the tail and your front foot straight across the middle of the board.
2. Snap the tail as you would for a normal ollie except scoop it a little behind you at the same time.

3. As you snap and scoop, lift your legs so that the board turns 180.
4. Land with your feet on the board after it finishes turning.
5. Your knees should be bent to absorb the impact as

you land.

The secrets to this trick are to scoop and pop, almost as if you were doing an ollie, and to lift your legs as the board ascends so that it can spin.

16 **Backside pop shuvit** (varial)

1. Place your back foot in the middle of the tail and your front foot straight across the board. Some people find it easier to hang the toes of the front foot slightly off the board.

2. Snap the tail like you would an ollie but scoop your back foot out in front of you in order to make the board spin 180.

3. As you snap and scoop with your back foot, be sure to lift your front foot up so that the board has the

freedom to spin.

4. As the board finishes the 180 and you begin your descent, place your feet on the board.

5. Land on the board with your knees slightly bent.

The secret to this trick is to keep the board from going too far behind you as it spins.

17 Backside 180 kickflip

1. Place your back foot in the middle of the tail. Your front foot should be a few inches higher than the middle of the board.

2. Snap the ollie, and in one fluid motion, turn your

shoulders and scoop the board so that you and the board begin to turn 180.

3. As the board begins to turn 180, flick your front foot across the board. If you are regular-footed, that will be across to the left. Goofy foots cross to the right.

4. The board should now be flipping and turning 180, simultaneously.

5. As you begin your descent, you should be facing backward. Keep your feet above the board as it flips.

6. Descend, place your feet on the board and land with knees bent for absorption.

The secret of backside flips is to perfect the flick of your front foot. It helps to flick it near the beginning of the 180 in order to bring the board completely around. Also remember that shoulder movement is crucial to swinging both your body and board around.

18 Frontside 180 kickflip

1. Place your back foot on the corner of the tail — left side for regular and right side for goofy.

2. Your front foot should be in the middle of the board at a 90-degree angle.

3. Before you pop the tail, start turning your shoulders so they are about at a 90-degree angle.

4. Snap the tail against the ground, and as you ascend, flick your front foot across and backward.

5. Your foot should follow your shoulders across and

around so that your body turns 180. Your shoulders should be a bit ahead of your feet, but by the end of the rotation, your feet catch up.

6. As you flick and rotate, keep your feet above the board.

7. As you descend, place your feet on the board and land with knees bent.

The secret to this trick is to flick your foot around and out past the board so your foot can come around and up for the landing. You don't want your feet to hinder the turning and flipping of the board.

19 Varial kickflip

1. Place your back foot in the middle of the tail. Your front foot should be slightly angled and in the middle of the board.

2. As you snap the tail, scoop your foot back slightly.

If you scoop it too much, it will over rotate.

3. When the board begins to rotate, flick your foot to the side to cause the board to flip.

4. As the board flips and rotates, be sure to stay above the board.

5. As you begin to descend, place your feet on the board and bend your knees for absorption.

The secrets to this trick are to rotate your board like a regular varial and to flick it slightly so that it flips.

20 Nollie half cab kickflip

1. Place your front foot in the middle of the nose. Your back foot should be in the kickflip position.

2. Snap the nose, and as the board ascends, turn your shoulders and feet so that your body and board begin a

180 turn.
3. At that point, flick your back foot across and around so your board does a 180 and a kickflip.
4. The kickflip should finished by the time the board has turned 180.

Nollie half cab kickflip

5. Keep your feet above the board as it flips.
6. Land with both feet on the board and bend your knees for absorption.

The secret to this trick is in the half cab. Learn nollie half cab ollies as well as kickflips first. Remember, the turning begins in the shoulders and feet, and the body follows.

21 Nollie backside kickflip

1. Place your front foot near the edge of the nose. If regular, use the right side of the nose, if goofy, the left.
2. Position your back foot at a 45-degree angle near the back of the bolts.

3. As you nollie, push the board forward and begin turning your shoulders.

4. When the board and body begin to turn 180, flick your back foot across and around so that your back leg lands in front.

5. As your board and body spin, suck your legs up so the board can flip under you.
6. Land with knees slightly bent.

The secret to this trick is the balance between your front and back foot. The trick requires a solid nollie 180 combined with a proper flick of the back foot.

22 Frontside 180 heelflip

1. Place your back foot near the edge of the tail. Left side for regular foot and right side for goofy.

2. Your front foot should be in the middle of the board with toes slightly overhanging.

3. As you crouch down to snap the tail, begin turning your shoulders 90 degrees.

4. As you ascend, scoop your back foot around so that your board and feet begin the 180.

5. When the board begins the 180, kick your front foot

across and bring it around with the rest of your body to complete the 180.

6. Suck your legs up so the board can flip underneath you without hindrance.

7. Land with your knees slightly bent.

The secret to this trick is the combination of the turning of the shoulders, the scoop of the back foot, and the kick and turn of the front foot. All three actions combine to make the body and board perform the trick.

23 Backside 180 heelflip

1. Place your back foot in the middle of the tail. Your front foot should be in the middle of the board with your toes hanging slightly over the edge.

2. Snap and scoop the tail so that your board begins to

turn 180.

3. As you scoop the tail, turn your shoulders so that both your feet and your shoulders are turning during the ascent.

4. As your board begins to turn, kick your front foot

straight across the board so that it flips. While the board is flipping, bring your legs up so that you are above the board.

5. Bend your knees for the landing.

The secret to this trick is to perfect your backside 180s and heelflips before you attempt this combination.

24 Fakie big spin heelflip

1. Ride backward and place your back foot on the side of the tail. If you skate regular, it will be the right side; goofy will be left.

2. Your front foot will be in the middle of the board

with your toes hanging slightly over the edge.

3. Snap the tail down and kick it out behind you to begin the 360 spin.

4. When you snap the tail, turn your shoulders.

5. Kick your back foot straight across the board like the

motion you use for heelflips.

6. As your body turns 180, your board should be flipping and spinning 360.

7. Land with knees bent.

The secret to this trick is to spin the board hard enough to get it around the full 360 degrees.

25 Nollie frontside 180 heelflip

1. Place your front foot on the nose with your toes near the front edge of the tail.

2. Your back foot should be in the middle of the board with your toes hanging slightly off the edge.

3. As you snap your nollie, turn your shoulders and bring your front foot around with the board.
4. As your board and body begin turning, kick your back foot out across the board so that the ball of your foot makes the board spin.

5. As the board spins and flips, bring your feet up so you do not interfere with its rotation.
6. Land with your knees bent.

The secret to this trick is popping a good nollie 180 so that board is in the air long enough to make it turn and flip.

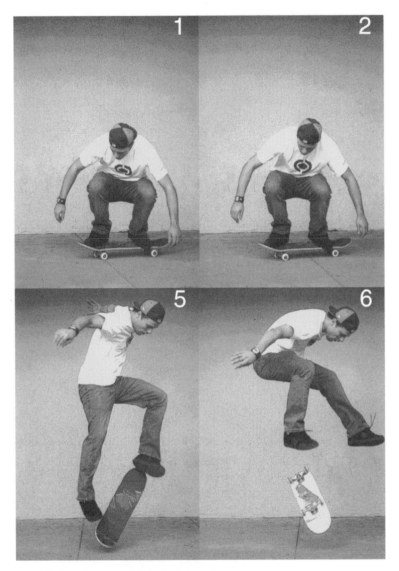

26 Nollie backside 180 heelflip

1. Place your front foot toward the left side of the tail for regular and toward the right side for goofy.

2. Your back foot should be at a 90-degree angle with your toes hanging slightly over the edge.

3. As you ride forward you will snap the nose, and in
one fluid motion, turn your shoulders and kick your
front foot out and around to the front of the board.
4. The kick of the board is like a heelflip but instead of
kicking straight out, you kick your foot out and around

to make 180 degrees.
5. As the board turns 180, turn with it. Place your feet on the board as you land 180.
6. Remember to land with your knees slightly bent for absorption.

The secret to nollie half cab heelflips is to kick your back foot out and around so that the board does a 180.

27 Hardflip

1. Place your back foot close to the side of the tail (regular will be the left side, goofy will be the right side).
2. Your front foot should be at a 90-degree angle with your toes close to the edge.

3. As you snap the tail, scoop it away from you so that your board does a varial.

4. As soon as the board pops up and begins to turn, flick your front foot out and around. Your front foot should look like it is doing a frontside flip while your

upper body stays straight.

5. Your front foot and the scoop of the back foot will cause the board to do a frontside flip.

6. Bring your legs up so the board can spin and turn under your feet.

7. Land with your knees bent.

The secret of this trick is to make the board do a frontside flip by shuvit-ing and flicking it while keeping your body straight.

28 Nollie big spin

1. Place your front foot on the side of the nose (left side for regular and right for goofy).
2. Put your back foot in the middle of the board with toes hanging slightly over the edge.

3. Snap the nose down and kick it out in front of you to begin the 360 spin.

4. Turn your shoulders as soon as you snap the nose.

5. Kick your back foot straight across the board as you would for a heelflip.

6. As your body turns 180, your board should be flipping and spinning 360. Land with knees sightly bent.

The secret of this trick is to spin the board hard enough to get it around a full 360 degrees.

29 Switch inward heelflip

1. Riding switch, take your front foot and hang your toes off the edge of the board. Your back foot should be in the ollie position.

2. As you snap the tail, scoop the board so it does a

142

shuvit.

3. As the board shuvits up, kick your front foot out so that the ball of your foot makes the board do a heelflip.

4. The scoop of the tail and the heelflip should cause the board to flip and turn.

5. As the board is rotating, bring your feet up so that the board can spin under you.

6. After the board completes its turn, land with your feet over the bolts.

The secret to this trick is in the pop shuvit. The higher you can pop this part of the trick, the easier it is to make the board rotate and flip.

30 Fakie inward big spin heelflip

1. Riding fakie, place your back foot on the edge of the tail. If you skate regular, it will be the right side of the tail; if goofy, it will be the left side.

2. Your front foot should be at a 45-degree angle with

your toes hanging slightly over the edge.

3. As you snap the tail, scoop it hard so the board will have enough momentum to turn a full 360 degrees.

4. Board and body should begin turning 180.

5. As the board and body begin the rotation, use your

back foot to heelflip the board by kicking your foot across it and bringing it around.

6. As the board flips and turns, continue to turn your body to complete a 180.

The secret to this trick is to get the board to spin a fakie 360 shuvit. Practice your inward heelflips and half cab heelflips.

Resources / Evan's picks

DC Shoe Co USA
DC Shoes has been around for quite some time and has some of the best riders in the world. Their Web site hosts recent skateboard news as well as some awesome skateboard footage.
www.dcshoecousa.com

Metro Clothes
Evan has started his own clothing company called Metro Clothes. Check out the Web site and buy some shirts off it.
www.metrofoundation.net

Skateboard Village
Skateboard Village is a Web site dedicated to posting chat rooms for skateboarders and snow-boarders. Skateboarders can post their glory shots for the world to see.
www.skateboardvillage.com

Slap Magazine
Slap Magazine is another skateboard magazine like *Transworld* and *Thrasher*. It can also be found in skateshops and convenience stores.
www.slapmagazine.com

Thrasher Magazine
Thrasher Magazine features Northern California skateboarding and special articles devoted to both punk and hip-hop music. This magazine is sold at most skateshops and convenience stores.
www.thrashermagazine.com

Transworld Skateboarding Magazine
This is a great magazine for those wanting to stay current with all the latest skateboard news, tricks and culture. It's available at almost every book store and convenience store.
www.skateboarding.com

United Riders Clothing
United Clothing is a skateboard clothing company that sponsors really good skateboarders. Check out there Web site and watch mayhem and skateboard footage. www.united-riders.com

Zero Skateboards
Zero skateboards is home to some of the best upcoming amateurs and pros. The Web site has interviews with riders, pictures and footage.
www.zeroskate.com

Zion Skateboards
Zion Skateboards is a skateboard company based in Vancouver, B.C., Canada. Evan currently rides for them and recommends their skateboards because of the quality and price. Check out there Web site and watch footage of Evan.
www.zionskate.com

Resources / comprehensive

For a quick fix go to **www.skateboarding.com** — an informative (but not the only) portal into the skateboarding galaxy.

Books
Discovered on **amazon.com** and **barnesandnoble.com**.

Baccigaluppi, John. *Declaration of Independents*. San Francisco, California: Chronicle Books, 2001.

Bermudez, Ben. *Skate! The Mongo's Guide to Skateboarding*. New York, New York: Cheapskate Press, 2001.

Borden, Ian. *Skateboarding, Space and the City*. New York, New York: Berg, 2001.

Brooke, Michael. *The Concrete Wave: The History of Skateboarding*. Toronto, Ontario: Warwick Publishing, 1999.

Burke, L.M. *Skateboarding! Surf the Pavement*. New York, New York: Rosen Publishing Group, Inc., 1999.

Davis, James. *Skateboard Roadmap*. England: Carlton Books Limited, 1999.

Gould, Marilyn. *Skateboarding*. Mankato, Minnesota: Capstone Press, 1991.

Gutman, Bill. *Skateboarding: To the Extreme*. New York, New York: Tom Doherty Associates, Inc., 1997.

Hawk, Tony. *Hawk*. New York, New York: Regan Books, 2001.

Powell, Ben. *Extreme Sports: Skateboarding*. Hauppauge, New York: Barron's Educational Series, Inc., 1999.

Riggins, Edward. *Ramp Plans*. San Francisco, California: High Speed Productions, 2000.

Ryan, Pat. *Extreme Skateboarding*. Mankato, Minnesota: Capstone Press, 1998.

Shoemaker, Joel. *Skateboarding Streetstyle*. Mankato, Minnesota: Capstone Press, 1995.

Thrasher. *Insane Terrain*. New York, New York: Universe Publishing, 2001.

Camps
Donny Barley Skate Camp
1747 West Main Road
Middletown, Rhode Island
02842
401-848-8078

Lake Owen
HC 60 Box 60
Cable, Wisconsin 54821
715-798-3785

Magdalena Ecke Family YMCA
200 Saxony Road
Encinitas, California 92023-0907
760-942-9622

Mission Valley YMCA
5505 Friars Road
San Diego, California 92110
619-298-3576

Skatelab
Steve Badillo Skate Camp
4226 Valley Fair Street
Simi Valley, California 93063
805-578-0040
vtaskate@aol.com

Snow Valley
PO Box 2337
Running Springs, California
92382
909-867-2751

Visalia YMCA
Sequoia Lake, California
211 West Tulare Avenue
Visalia, California 93277
559-627-0700

Woodward Camp
Box 93
Route 45
Woodward, Pennsylvania 16882
814-349-5633

Young Life Skate Camp
Hope, British Columbia, Canada
604-807-3718

Magazines
Big Brother
www.bigbrothermagazine.com

Skateboarder
Surfer Publications
PO Box 1028
Dana Point, California 92629

Thrasher
High Speed Productions
1303 Underwood Avenue
San Francisco, California 94124
415-822-3083
www.thrashermagazine.com

Transworld Skateboarding
353 Airport Road
Oceanside, California 92054
760-722-7777
www.skateboarding.com

Museums
Huntington Beach International
Skate and Surf Museum
411 Olive Street
Huntington Beach, California
714-960-3483

Skatelab
4226 Valley Fair
Simi Valley, California
805-578-0040
www.skatelab.com

Skatopia
34961 Hutton Road
Rutland, Ohio 45775
740-742-1110

Organizations, movers, shakers . . .
Action Sports Retailer
Organizer of the Action Sports
Retailer Trade Expos
949-376-8144
www.asrbiz.com

California Amateur Skateboard
League (CASL) and PSL
Amateur and professional
contest organizer
909-883-6176
Fax 909-883-8036

The Canadian Cup
416-960-2222

Extreme Downhill International
1666 Garnet Avenue #308
San Diego, California 92109
619-272-3095

International Association of
Skateboard Companies (IASC)
PO Box 37
Santa Barbara, California 93116
805-683-5676
Fax 805-967-7537
iascsk8@aol.com
www.skateboardiasc.org

International Network
for Flatland Freestyle
Skateboarding
Abbedissavagen 15
746 95 Balsta, Sweden

KC Projects
Canadian amateur contest
organizer
514-806-7838
kc_projects@aol.com
5148067838@fido.ca

National Amateur Skateboard
Championships
Damn Am Series
National amateur contest
organizer
813-621-6793
www.skateparkoftampa.com
www.nascseries.com

National Skateboarders
Association of Australia (NSAA)
Amateur and professional
contest organizers
61-2-9878-3876
www.skateboard.asn.au

The Next Cup
Southern California amateur
contest organizer
858-874-4970 ext. 114 or 129
www.thenextcup.com

Real Amateur Skateboarding
Amateur contest organizer
619-501-1341
realamateurskateboarding
@hotmail.com

Skateboarding Association of
America
Amateur contest organizer
727-523-0875
www.skateboardassn.org

Skatepark Association of the
USA (SPAUSA)
Resource for skatepark
planning/operating
310-823-9228
www.spausa.org

Southwest Sizzler
Southwestern amateur contest
organizer
918-638-6492

Surf Expo
East Coast trade show
800-947-SURF
www.surfexpo.com

United Skateboarding
Association (USA)
Skate event organizer
and action sport marketing/
promotions
732-432-5400
ext. 2168 and 2169
www.unitedskate.com

Vans Shoes
Organizer of the Triple Crown
skate events
562-565-8267
www.vans.com

World Cup Skateboarding
Organizer of some of skating's
largest events
530-888-0596
Fax 530-888-0296
danielle@wcsk8.com
www.wcsk8.com

Zeal Skateboarding Association
Southern California amateur
contest organizer
909-265-3420
www.zealsk8.com

**Public skateparks /
information about building
and starting up**

Consolidated Skateboards
(see *The Plan*)
www.consolidatedskateboard
.com

International Association of
Skateboard Companies (IASC)
PO Box 37
Santa Barbara, California 93116
805-683-5676
Fax 805-967-7537
iascsk8@aol.com
www.skateboardiasc.org

Skatepark Association of the
USA (SPAUSA)
310-823-9228
www.spausa.org

www.skatepark.org

**Public skatepark designers /
builders**
Airspeed Skateparks LLC
2006 Highway 101 #154
Florence, Oregon 97439
503-791-4674
airspeed@airspeedskateparks
.com
www.airspeedskateparks.com

CA Skateparks, Design/Build
and General Contracting
273 North Benson Avenue
Upland, California 91786
562-208-4646
www.skatedesign.com

Dreamland Skateparks,
Grindline, Inc.
4056 23rd Avenue SW
Seattle, Washington 98106
206-933-7915
www.grindline.com

Ramptech
www.ramptech.com

SITE Design Group, Inc.
414 South Mill Avenue,
Suite 210
Tempe, Arizona 85281
480-894-6797
Fax 480-894-6792
mm@sitedesigngroup.com
www.sitedesigngroup.com

Spectrum Skatepark
Creations, Ltd.
M/A 2856 Clifftop Lane
Whistler, B.C.
V0N 1B2 Canada
250-238-0140
design@spectrum-sk8.com
www.spectrum-sk8.com

Team Pain
864 Gazelle Trail
Winter Springs, Florida 32708
407-695-8215
tim@teampain.com
www.teampain.com

John Woodstock Designs
561-743-5963
johnwoodstock@msn.com
www.woodstockskateparks.com

**Shops / skateparks
finding one close to you**
Two (among quite a few) that
will help:
www.skateboarding.com
www.skateboards.org

Television
ESPN
X Games
espn.go.com/extreme

NBC
Gravity Games
www.gravitygames.com

Web sites
www.board-trac.com
Market researchers for skateboarding industry.

www.bigbrother.com
A comprehensive site by *Big
Brother* magazine.

www.exploratorium.edu/
skateboarding
Glossary, scientific explanations
and equipment for skating.

www.interlog.com/~mbrooke/
skategeezer.html
International Longboarder
magazine.

www.ncdsa.com
Northern California Downhill
Skateboarding Association.

www.skateboardiasc.org
International Association of
Skateboard Companies (IASC) is
one of the leading advocates of
skateboarding progress and provides a wealth of information.

www.skateboard.com
Chat and messages.

www.skateboarding.com
Every skater's site by
Transworld Skateboarding
magazine.

www.skateboards.org
Find parks, shops and companies.

www.skatelab.com
One of Los Angeles area's
largest indoor parks and world's
largest skateboard museum.

www.skater.net
Skate parks and ramp plans.

www.smithgrind.com
Skate news wire.

www.switchmagazine.com
*Switch Skateboarding
Magazine.*

www.thrashermagazine.com
A comprehensive site by
Thrasher magazine.

Videos / Instructional

411 Video Productions. *The
First Step.*

411 Video Productions. *The
Next Step.*

Hawk, Tony. *Tony Hawk's Trick
Tips Volume I: Skateboarding
Basics.* 900 Films, 2001.

Hawk, Tony. *Tony Hawk's Trick
Tips Volume II: Essentials of
Street.* 900 Films, 2001.

Thrasher Magazine. *How to
Skateboard.* San Francisco,
California: High Speed
Productions, Inc., 1995.

Thrasher Magazine. *How to
Skateboard Better.* San
Francisco, California: High
Speed Productions, Inc., 1997.

Transworld Skateboarding.
Starting Point. Oceanside,
California, 1997.

Transworld Skateboarding. *Trick
Tips with Wily Santos.*
Oceanside, California, 1998.

Transworld Skateboarding.
Starting Point Number Two.
Oceanside, California, 1999.

Index

More skate guides from Tracks

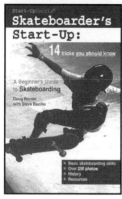

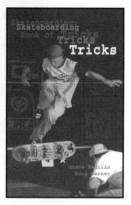

Skateboarder's Start-Up:
A Beginner's Guide to Skateboarding
$11.95
An essential start-up guide.

Skateboarding: New Levels
Tricks and Tips for Serious Riders
$12.95
Intermediate and advanced skating.

Skateboarding: Book of Tricks
$12.95
A look at old-school and new-school skateboarding.

Street Skateboarding: Endless Grinds and Slides
$12.95
Curb tricks galore.

Coming Spring 2006

Ramp Tricks

It's simple. Our skate guides are the most popular skate instructional books on the globe because they're inexpensive and contain hundreds of sequential images to explain the tricks you should know.

Available at all major bookstores and booksellers on the Internet.

About the author

Evan Goodfellow is a lifelong skater and skateboard instructor. He is the author of *Street Skateboarding: Endless Grinds and Slides* and is currently writing his third skate instructional guide, *Ramp Tricks*. Evan has also appeared in eight skate videos.

His sponsors have included Vans Shoes, Ambiguous Clothing, Zion Skateboards and Ninetimes Boardshop. He earned a master's degree in education from Biola University, La Mirada, California in 2004.

Evan is starting up a clothing company with a few friends. Check it out. www.metrofoundation.net.